Troubleshooting Tips
for
Your Breadmaker

Troubleshooting Tips
for
Your Breadmaker

Karen Saunders

EBURY PRESS
LONDON

First published by Ebury Publishing
Random House, 20 Vauxhall Bridge Road, London SW1V 2SA

Random House Australia (Pty) Limited
20 Alfred Street, Milsons Point, Sydney, New South Wales 2061, Australia

Random House New Zealand Limited
18 Poland Road, Glenfield, Auckland 10, New Zealand

Random House South Africa (Pty) Limited
Endulini, 5A Jubilee Road, Parktown 2193, South Africa

The Random House Group Limited Reg. No. 954009
www.randomhouse.co.uk

A CIP catalogue record for this book is available from the British Library.
ISBN 0091909120

Editor: Gillian Haslam
Designer: Christine Wood
Illustrations: Lizzie Collcutt

Printed and bound in Great Britain by
Mackays of Chatham plc, Chatham, Kent

contents

introduction

'Help! Quick! The dough is lifting the lid of my machine. Oh... Now it's started coming down the sides – what should I do?'

Of the thousands of phone calls, letters and emails I've answered from breadmaker owners, it's this chap I remember the most. Panicked and anxious, the portrayal of his imminent drowning by bread dough conjured up a vision in my mind fit for any horror movie. Rest assured that the mistake was a simple one and once the contents of the breadmaker had been successfully eliminated, his next loaf was perfectly contained.

Using a breadmaker is easy. By its very nature, the machine is designed to do the hard work for you. And it does. But unfortunately there is still not a machine that can fill itself. It's up to us to take charge of what goes in and it's here that we often make the simple mistakes that result in disappointing loaves.

If, like many of us, you're not the sort to read every word of the instruction manual before you start, it's likely that you go straight for the first recipe, hurriedly tip in the ingredients and press start. On returning 3–4 hours later, it's probable that your bread isn't quite what was expected and then you resort to trying to discover what it is you've done wrong. I prefer to take a more positive approach and for breadmakers this needn't mean hours of reading. There are a few golden rules (see below) that should never be broken and sticking to these is the secret of success.

So, whether you've just unwrapped your breadmaker for the first time or you're a seasoned baker striving to make even better loaves, this little book is for you. It will help you every step of the way, explaining the simple golden rules, giving tried-and-tested recipes and encouraging you to expand your repertoire. And, if things don't quite turn out as you'd hoped, the step-by-step troubleshooting chapter on page 117 will get you back on track in no time.

Happy baking!

the four golden rules
Choose the right yeast (see page 29)
Measure your ingredients properly (see page 37)
Add ingredients in the right order (see page 38)
Have a look! (see page 39)

introduction

getting
started

- *Getting to Know Your Breadmaker*
- *Location, Location*
- *Manufacturer's Instructions*

getting to know your breadmaker

Take a little time to get to know your breadmaker and its constituent parts. Understanding how it all fits together and what each part is for will make the whole process easier, and will also increase your confidence when using the machine. Refer to the manufacturer's handbook and use the quick reference guide below to help you.

measuring cup and spoon

Most machines come with a plastic measuring cup and spoon. These can be used for measuring both wet and dry ingredients. Always use this spoon for all teaspoon and tablespoon measuring – never use household cutlery. Most recipes give alternatives for measuring in standard grams or ounces (measured with kitchen scales) and cups (using the cup provided). Choose whichever method you are most comfortable with and stick to it – never mix the two.

breadmaker bucket

Depending on your particular model, this non-stick bucket fits into the machine either by using a simple twist action or by pressing it down into the unit until it clicks in place. It's well worth practising removing the bucket a few times while the breadmaker is cold so that when you need to remove a hot loaf with oven gloves, you are familiar with the mechanism.

Always remove the bucket from the machine to add ingredients as this will prevent spillage into the inner cavity and stop ingredients burning onto the elements.

kneading blade

The blade fits securely onto the shaft in the centre of the bucket and has a non-stick surface. Some larger machines have two blades and these work in exactly the same way. Before making your first loaf, practise fitting the blade onto the shaft to ensure it is securely connected so that it can efficiently mix and knead the dough. **note:** In some models, the blade is not removable and is permanently secured to the shaft (refer to your manufacturer's handbook).

ingredient dispenser

Some machines have added ingredient dispensers in the lid. These activate automatically during the cycle to add delicate ingredients (e.g. fruit or nuts) to the dough as it is kneading. Adding ingredients later in the cycle ensures the paddle does not break them up too finely while the dough is mixing.

window, lid and vents

Most machines have a viewing window that allows you to see what is happening during the cycle. If your machine does not have a viewing facility, lift the lid occasionally while the dough is mixing or kneading to check the consistency. With some models the lid is removable to make cleaning easier.

Check the position of the vents on your machine. During the baking cycle these may puff out steam, so ensure that adequate room is left around your machine to allow this steam to escape safely.

location, location

In general, keep your machine in a dry and draught-free place at a comfortable room temperature. Never keep it outside or in the garage, and never place it in direct sunlight or next to the hob or oven. Ensure there is ample space around and above your machine for air to circulate and that the air vents are not obstructed. Take care when the machine is baking as the outside can get quite hot and the air vents can puff out steam.

Even though breadmakers control the environment in which your bread is made, the external environment can still affect them. So bear in mind that if a trusted recipe suddenly fails, it could simply be due to turning the central heating on or the fact that the weather is very hot and humid.

manufacturer's instructions

If you are new to baking with a breadmaker, take the time to read the hints and tips in this book and in your manufacturer's handbook before you start. Practise first with basic loaves until you are familiar with the way your machine works and how your bread will look at all the various stages before moving on to more advanced recipes.

using your breadmaker

- The Baking Process
- What Are the Cycles For?
- Cleaning Your Breadmaker

the baking process

Have you ever wondered how your breadmaker works, and which stages make up every cycle and what the difference is between the cycles themselves? Understanding how dough and bread are made and how this is reflected in breadmaker programmes will help you to judge your dough better as it is mixing and kneading. This, in turn, means that you are able to correct any slight variations in consistency before it's too late.

In very basic terms, your breadmaker will mix, knead, prove, rise and bake your dough, i.e. you put in the ingredients and, later, take out a loaf of bread – there's nothing more for you to do.

Your manufacturer's handbook may provide a breakdown of every programme to show you the amount of time given to each stage, so you can see for yourself how the different programmes vary. Most programmes are made up of the following stages:

rest/preheat

A rest period is not included in every cycle or every model, and indeed it may seem odd to start a programme with nothing obvious happening. So, rest assured that if you turn your machine on and it doesn't start mixing straight away, it probably has a 'rest' stage at the beginning of the cycle. During this time the machine is gently warming the ingredients to bring them to the optimum temperature for the yeast to start working once mixing begins.

mixing

Just as if by hand, the machine combines all the ingredients together by mixing. This usually involves a combination of intermittent pulses and continuous mixing by the machine, so expect changes in the sound of the machine while this stage is taking place.

kneading

Once mixing is complete the machine will run non-stop, mixing the ball of dough continuously and kneading it. During this stage the mix is transformed from an uneven mass into a smooth, slightly tacky dough. As it is moved around inside the bucket, any excess pockets of flour should be incorporated into the mix, leaving the interior of the bucket almost clean.

Some programmes have two kneading stages with a short rest period in between. It is in the final kneading stage that 'Added Ingredients' are usually incorporated. If your breadmaker doesn't have an automatic dispenser for this, a 'bleep' can usually be heard during

using your breadmaker

the second kneading cycle to indicate that this is the time for any extra ingredients (e.g. dried fruit or nuts) to be added (see page 41).

Quick Tip

In some recipes it may be necessary to scrape excess flour into the mix/dough from the sides of the bucket while the dough is mixing or kneading. This is especially true when making gluten-, wheat- or yeast-free bread or cakes, as the dough is not so elastic and is more cake-like. I use a long-handled, small, plastic spatula for this purpose (intended for scraping the last bit of sauce from the bottom of the tomato ketchup bottle!).

rising/rest

When making bread by hand, the dough is always left in a warm place after kneading to encourage fermentation. During this time gas bubbles are trapped in the dough, causing the dough to rise. Your breadmaker automatically creates exactly the right environment for optimum fermentation, encouraging the best possible rise. The machine is silent while rising and you may notice that the outer casing becomes slightly warm.

knock back/knock down

When the dough has risen once, a traditional baker would 'knock back' the dough by punching it and using a short, quick kneading action. This process helps break up any large pockets of air and produces a more even and satisfying texture in the finished loaf. Your breadmaker does the same process for you with a few quick flicks of the paddle between rising cycles.

second rise

Once the dough has been knocked back, it is left to rise for a second time. Breadmakers automatically vary the length of time given to this second rise to reflect the composition of different bread varieties, with wholewheat and French programmes generally giving a much longer rise than the basic/white programme.

bake

Your breadmaker automatically switches from rise to baking mode and controls the temperature and timing of this process for the composition and size of loaf as dictated by your cycle selection. During this cycle the sides of the machine may become hot and steam may puff out of the vents, so take care when near the breadmaker.

using your breadmaker

At the end of the baking process a 'bleep' will sound to signal the end of the cycle. Using oven gloves, carefully remove your finished loaf from the breadmaker.

keep warm

Some machines offer a 'keep warm' function that keeps the bread warm for a predetermined length of time once the cycle has finished. Most claim that this process also prevents the bread from going soggy, but in my experience the bread is best removed from the machine as soon as the baking cycle has finished.

what are the cycles for?

Here's a quick, at-a-glance guide to the different cycles offered by your breadmaker.

basic/normal/white

For producing standard loaves made mainly from white, soft grain or brown flour.

wholewheat

For making loaves made from a blend of heavier wholemeal (wholewheat) flours and for recipes using grains such as oats and rye. This programme generally allows a longer rise time more suited to heavier doughs.

french

When used to make French bread recipes, this cycle will produce the distinctive light, airy interior and golden, crispy crust.

quick bread

For making quick yeast loaves. Generally one of the rising cycles is skipped in this programme, which means that loaves may not rise so well as those made on standard cycles.

rapid/turbo

As with the quick bread programme (above), kneading and rising time is reduced to a minimum, allowing you to make bread much more quickly but often with the side effect of a less well-risen loaf.

sweet

This programme is designed for sweet bread recipes and gives a lower baking temperature to prevent over-browning or scorching the crust.

Quick Tip

Try the sweet programme if you prefer a softer crust on your standard loaves.

cake

No kneading or rising is included in this cycle, which is designed simply to mix and bake cake mixtures.

gluten-/yeast-free

Designed for gluten- and yeast-free breads that do not require the lengthy kneading and rising periods of standard yeast loaves.

dough

For mixing and preparing light, airy doughs that can be finished and baked in the conventional way. With most breadmakers the cycle finishes after the kneading stage, although some dough programmes include rising time too.

bake

This is generally a programmable option that is used either to extend the baking time of a loaf after a cycle has finished, or to bake breads and cakes when you want to use the baking part of the cycle only, to save heating your conventional oven.

jam

For making jam in your breadmaker! Follow your manufacturer's handbook for quantities and the method for your particular machine.

As bread machines become more complex, the functions include specific programmes for an ever wider range of breads. For convenience, I have used programmes that are universal to the majority of machines on the market. There's nothing to stop you experimenting with the other programmes – simply follow your manufacturer's handbook and adjust the recipe if necessary.

cleaning your breadmaker

Before cleaning your breadmaker, always unplug the unit and allow it to cool completely.

body and lid

Any crumbs or particles that have collected in the base of the cavity can be easily removed using the hose of your vacuum cleaner. The body and lid should then be wiped clean with a damp cloth, using only a mild detergent if necessary.

For baked-on deposits use a non-scratch scourer or detergent. NEVER use steel wool or other abrasive pads and cleaners.

If your machine has an 'Added Ingredients' dispenser, also wipe this clean with a damp cloth after every use to prevent an unhygienic build-up of residues.

bread bucket and paddle

Looking after the non-stick coating on your breadmaker bucket and paddle is the most important piece of maintenance you can give your machine. NEVER be tempted to use metal utensils to remove loaves from the bucket or to remove the paddle from bread as these will scratch and damage the surface.

After making each loaf, simply wipe the pan clean with a damp cloth. If any baked dough remains around the paddle, cover the base of the bucket with warm water and a mild detergent and leave to soak for 10–15 minutes, after which time you should be able to clean it easily with a soft cloth.

NEVER PUT YOUR BREADMAKER BUCKET OR PADDLE IN THE DISHWASHER.

Quick Tip

If the paddle gets stuck in the bottom of your bread, carefully remove it with a pair of plastic kitchen tongs, taking care not to damage the non-stick surface of the paddle, or your bread. It's worth noting that most manufacturers sell extra paddles and buckets if needed.

plastic cup and spoon

Wash in warm soapy water and wipe dry.

basic ingredients

- What is Bread?
- Flour • Yeast • Salt • Sugar •
- Fat • Liquid
- Storage and Freezing Tips

what is bread?

Bread is a combination of flour, yeast and water. In most recipes salt and a sweetener (usually either sugar or honey) are also added to assist the action of the yeast. These two ingredients are essential in breadmaker loaves to ensure the yeast works properly within the confines of the regulated cycles.

Understanding the contribution that each basic ingredient makes to the loaf will help you to develop confidence in adjusting recipes to suit your taste, and will also mean that you will often be able to correct any inconsistencies in your dough at the mixing stage, before the bread is baked.

flour
wheat flours

To achieve the best results, high-protein flour made from 'hard' or 'strong' wheat should be used. Always look for the word 'strong' on the packaging. Standard plain or self-raising flours are not suitable for breadmaking.

When dough made from strong flour is kneaded, the protein from the flour develops into gluten. Gluten is the elastic substance that forms the mesh-like structure that encapsulates the carbon dioxide bubbles given off by the fermenting yeast. It is this gluten structure that allows the dough to develop, making the light and airy texture of fresh cooked bread.

common strong wheat flours
strong white bread flour

This is the classic white bread flour that, during milling, has the bran and germ removed giving a flour of approximately 70–75 per cent extraction. (The term extraction simply refers to the percentage of the whole grain typically used in the flour.)

very strong white bread flour

This premium white bread flour is blended from the finest hard wheat varieties, usually imported from Canada and North America, to produce a flour super-high in gluten. It can be used wherever a recipe calls for strong white bread flour and will generally help to give a better volume and lighter results. I find this flour particularly useful for giving improved rise and texture to loaves made with a blend of flours including those that are denser or naturally low in gluten, such as wholemeal and rye.

wholesome white very strong bread flour

Made with a new variety of 'white' wheat, this innovative flour is a mix of strong white bread flour and strong white wheat wholemeal flour. When used in a breadmaker, it will give a wonderfully light loaf with a 'rustic' creamy-coloured interior that contains the goodness of a wholemeal flour.

strong wholemeal flour

To be called wholemeal, this flour must be of 100 per cent extraction. This means that the whole grain is used in its production, including the germ and bran. Thus the full nutritional value of the grain is retained, making this flour a useful source of B vitamins, calcium, iron and fibre. However, the presence of bran reduces the effectiveness of gluten during baking; hence bread made with wholemeal flour will not rise as high and will be much denser than its white equivalent. The presence of bran also means that the flour will absorb more liquid, so more water is needed in the dough when wholemeal flour is used.

When using wholemeal flour in a breadmaker, I would always recommend only using it as 50 per cent of the total flour mix. A 50:50 blend with 50 per cent strong white flour or very strong white flour will produce a better texture and a much lighter loaf.

basic ingredients

strong brown flour

Brown flour is different to wholemeal flour in that it is of 90 per cent extraction, i.e. 10 per cent of the bran is omitted. Brown flour is high in nutrients and will still absorb slightly more liquid than white flour. However, it will produce a noticeably lighter loaf than wholemeal, hence it is possible to make excellent 100 per cent brown loaves in a breadmaker.

country grain strong brown bread flour

A base of strong brown flour enhanced with malted wheat flakes. This flour is also known as malted wheat grain or granary.

soft grain strong white bread flour

Strong white flour with added fibre due to the addition of cracked wheat and rye grains, that also give the bread an interesting texture and additional 'bite'.

other flours used in breadmaking

It's not only wheat-based flours that can be used for breadmaking. For thousands of years flours ground from many dried grains, roots and seeds have been used in bread, from barley, rye, maize and millet to flours made from potatoes or chickpeas. These non-wheat flours tend to have little or no gluten and, therefore, cannot be used alone to make bread in a breadmaker. They can, however, be blended with strong wheat flours to vary the taste and texture of bread. My book *The Breadmaker Bible* (see page 140) gives recipes for many of these flours, showing how they can be used to make a wide range of tasty breads using complete breadmaker cycles.

yeast

Confusion over which type of yeast to use in breadmakers is, without any doubt, the biggest area of mystery for new bread-machine owners. So, if you only remember one fact about yeast, make it this: only use instant or fast-acting yeast (also called easy-bake yeast) in your breadmaker.

Instant, fast-acting or easy-bake yeast is widely available in sachets and also in larger packs that are more convenient if you bake everyday. This yeast is made by removing the moisture from fresh yeast (making it inactive) and drying it. The yeast is compressed to give very fine particles that do not need to go through the rehydration process before being added to the dough mixture. With some brands, the presence of vitamin C (ascorbic acid) – a natural dough improver – also helps ensure the fast action of the yeast and works to improve the protein structure, helping the dough to trap carbon dioxide and rise more effectively.

Pay attention to the storage and use-by information printed on the yeast packaging and don't be tempted to save partially used sachets for your next baking session – the yeast will become inactive and your bread will not rise.

Do not use fresh yeast in your breadmaker, and although some manufacturers' handbooks insist on recommending traditional dried active yeast (the type usually sold in tins), I would not recommend it as the easiest option for use in a breadmaker. Dried active yeast is designed for traditional hand baking and is best used only for this particular purpose.

how does yeast work?

Yeast is a living organism and should always be treated as such. Like us, it requires food and warmth to grow and will die if it gets too cold. Yeast is needed to turn bread from a solid mass of dough into an air-filled spongy mass that, once baked, will be a delight to eat. The process involved is known as fermentation.

During fermentation, yeast is activated by liquid and feeds on sugar and the starch from the flour. As it grows, the yeast gives off carbon dioxide and alcohol. When this happens in bread dough, the gas bubbles get caught in the mesh-like gluten structure and rise until finally the heat of the oven kills off the yeast and the starch in the flour sets, holding the shape of the risen loaf.

When making bread traditionally, you can judge when optimum fermentation has been achieved and bake the dough, but when using a breadmaker the time of the cycles is strictly regulated. This means careful measuring of the ingredients (see page 37) and the use of salt (see below) are the only factors that control the action of the yeast.

salt

Salt serves to control the action of the yeast throughout the baking process, gives a well-rounded flavour to the bread and improves the keeping qualities of the loaf. Salt should be used with care as adding too much will kill the yeast and too little will mean that the dough could rise out of control, so always measure carefully.

I'm often asked about leaving salt out of bread but in my experience, especially in a breadmaker, salt-free dough tends to over-rise, giving a poor-quality loaf and a collapsed crust. If you're trying to cut down on salt in your diet remember that, compared to processed foods, home-made bread is very low in salt. Wherever possible, I use the minimum amount of salt in my recipes, so turn your attention to reducing the salt content of the foods you serve with your bread. For more information see page 115.

sugar

Most breadmaker recipes use sugar to give the yeast a quick supply of food to ensure sufficient fermentation occurs within the limits of the machine's cycle.

Be aware that too much sugar will kill the yeast. Particular care should be taken with recipes that use more than one sweet ingredient (e.g. syrup, chocolate, fruit, jam or chutney) as collectively the total sugar content could destroy the yeast.

fat

In our low-fat world it's often forgotten that butter or oil is added to bread to enhance its crumb structure, taste and keeping qualities.

Butter, margarine and vegetable oils can be substituted like for like to vary the flavour to suit your taste. Don't use low fat spreads unless they are designed for baking. Flavoured oils are especially useful for providing additional taste, and olive oil adds a wonderful touch.

liquid

Almost any liquid can be used to bind bread dough. While water is the usual choice, milk, cream, buttermilk or natural yoghurt can all be used and loaves can also be made using beer, cold tea, juices and wine.

Whatever liquid is used, bear in mind that yeast is heat sensitive and the liquid should be added at the right temperature. Yeast will die if the liquid is too hot or cold. Most breadmakers gently heat the dough as it mixes so don't worry too much about accurately measuring the temperature with a thermometer to the last degree – simply ensure your ingredients are at room temperature when you begin.

basic ingredients

storage and freezing tips

flour

Flour should be stored in a cool, dry place – ideally in an airtight container. Pay attention to the use-by dates on packaging and always seal the top of the bag after use. If you only bake occasionally, flour is best stored in the freezer. Just ensure that the flour has time to reach room temperature before making bread with it. As wholemeal flour contains more fat than white, it does not keep as long as white flour.

yeast

See the notes on page 30 for storing and using yeast.

dough

If time is short, bread dough can be frozen for use later as long as it doesn't contain any ingredients that are either perishable or unsuitable for freezing. Seal unshaped dough in an oiled plastic bag, leaving just enough space for the dough to rise slightly as it freezes. Dough will keep for up to five days. To thaw, place the dough in the fridge for 12–24 hours, until it doubles in size. Remove from the fridge and shape, prove and bake as normal.

bread

Only store bread after it has thoroughly cooled. According to your preference, store bread in a clean dry cloth, a sealed plastic bag, or a bread bin at room temperature. Do not store bread in the fridge as this will dehydrate the bread and speed up the staling process.

Cooled baked bread can be frozen either wrapped in foil or a plastic freezer bag. Be sure to push all the air out of the bag before freezing. Bread can be frozen for up to 3 months, but ideally not longer than 3–4 weeks. For best results defrost bread slowly in a cool place or in the fridge for 8–10 hours, then store as above.

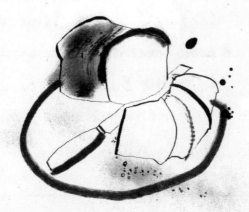

practice makes perfect

- How to Measure • Order of Ingredients
- Look, Feel and Listen
- Mastering Basic Recipes
- Added Ingredients
- Toppings and Glazes

how to measure

I've made literally thousands of breadmaker loaves over the years and I still measure all my ingredients every time; you should do the same.

When using a breadmaker it's essential to measure all your ingredients carefully and accurately. Either use the plastic cup provided with your machine, or metric or imperial measures. Follow one set of measurements only – never mix them.

Always use the plastic spoon provided for measuring all teaspoons and tablespoons. Never use household cutlery as the size of these varies enormously.

If you prefer to weigh ingredients, for the best results I strongly recommend investing in a set of electronic scales that can measure both liquid (ml/fl oz) and dry ingredients (g/oz). In most cases you can simply stand the breadmaker bucket on top of the scales and measure directly into it, which is much quicker and reduces the amount of washing-up too.

When using the plastic cup provided with your machine to measure dry ingredients, do not press ingredients down into the cup – simply level them off with a knife. Solid fats and other paste-like ingredients are the only ones that require pressing into the cup when measuring to ensure that all air pockets have been eliminated.

order of ingredients

The fundamental principle here is to keep the yeast well away from any moisture.

Always add the ingredients in the order specified for your particular model (check your manufacturer's handbook for this). Most machines put the wet ingredients in first, followed by the flour, then the yeast. Some machines advise the reverse – adding the yeast first and then the dry ingredients followed by the liquid. If your machine recommends this, when using the recipes in this book, simply reverse the order in which the ingredients are added to the bucket by reading from bottom to top in the recipes.

In both cases the main aim is to keep the yeast well away from the liquid, which is especially important if you are using the delay timer function. Remember that as soon as yeast meets moisture, it starts to activate and you don't want this to happen until your ingredients start mixing, in order to ensure that there is enough power left in the yeast to rise the bread.

Some breadmaker recipe books also recommend keeping the sugar and salt away from the yeast. If you get into the habit of adding liquid, sugar, salt, flour, then yeast (as in my recipes), or vice versa, then this is done naturally.

practice makes perfect

look, feel and listen

While breadmakers are fully automatic, the ability to correct any slight mistakes with the ingredients added by you is not. For this reason it is essential to keep an eye on your dough while it is mixing and kneading; after all, this is why most machines have a viewing window!

For most basic recipes your dough should be smooth, slightly tacky to the touch and slump just a little when the paddle stops turning. Dough becomes smoother as kneading progresses, which is why most manufacturers recommend making any necessary adjustments to flour or liquid during the second kneading cycle. If, however, your mix does not form a rough dough after the initial mixing cycle, it may be necessary to make adjustments earlier in the cycle (see page 15).

Ideally you should know how the cycles of your machine work, how the dough should look and feel at every stage, and also how the machine sounds. For example, can you tell whether your machine is kneading a stiff or soft dough by the sound of it? If you make a habit of listening and lifting the lid to feel the dough as it's worked you'll learn the characteristics of the best dough for your particular model. By doing this you'll be able to make any adjustments to recipes during the kneading cycles, should your dough be too wet or too dry, correcting any potential problems before it's too late.

practice makes perfect

In some recipes it may be necessary to scrape excess flour from the sides of the bucket into the mix/dough as the dough is mixing. This is especially true when making gluten-free or wheat-free bread, as the dough is not so elastic and more cake-like. I use a long-handled small, plastic spatula (intended for scraping the last bit of sauce from the ketchup bottle) for this purpose and it works a treat.

mastering basic recipes

If you are a newcomer to breadmaker baking, I would always recommend making the same basic loaf several times before progressing to the more complex recipes or flour combinations. In this way you'll quickly learn how the dough should look and how your machine sounds when kneading dough of the right consistency. Then, once you start varying the ingredients, you will know just what it is you are trying to achieve.

expanding your repertoire

Changing the flour you use to make your bread is the easiest way to add variety to your baking. Follow the basic recipes on pages 52–59 for guidance on how to incorporate these into your loaves.

The easiest way to expand your repertoire of recipes is to invest in a good breadmaker cookery book, such as *The Breadmaker Bible* or *Traditional Breads for your Breadmaker* (see page 140), and use this to guide you.

added ingredients

You can vary a basic recipe quickly and easily by adding extra ingredients like fruit and nuts to your dough. Herbs, spices, seeds and cheese can also be added with the other dry ingredients. Add softer ingredients, like dried or ready-to-eat fruit or nuts, during the second kneading cycle so they retain their shape and to prevent them getting mashed up by the paddle during mixing. See the list on the following page for suggested added ingredients.

Most machines sound a 'bleep' to signal when extra ingredients should be added and some models have a little trap door in the lid that automatically drops the additional ingredients in at the appropriate time. As you become more experienced in using your breadmaker, you will learn how best to add particular ingredients to suit your own tastes. Follow the instructions for adding extra ingredients in your manufacturer's handbook.

Here are some extra ingredients that can be added to basic recipes. (For a guide on quantities refer to your manufacturer's handbook, or as a rough guide use 1 cup of added ingredients to every 450 g/16 oz/ 3 cups of flour.)

- Nuts: walnuts, hazelnuts, almonds, pecans, unsalted cashews, peanuts.
- Seeds: sunflower, caraway, pumpkin, poppy, sesame, linseed.
- Dried fruit: raisins, sultanas, currants, chopped mixed peel.
- Roughly chopped semi-dried (ready-to-eat) fruit: apricots, prunes, mango, pineapple, apple, pear, cranberries, blueberries.
- Herbs/spices: 1–2 tsp dried herbs or spices.
- Other: dried onion flakes, chocolate chips.

notes:
- Some ingredients can spoil bread made in a breadmaker and so should be used with caution. I recommend following a fully tested recipe for quantities and advice on how they should be added.
- Ingredients to be wary of include: garlic, fresh onion, too much cheese, fresh herbs, watery vegetables (such as courgettes and spinach) and fresh fruit.

toppings and glazes

Adding toppings and glazes is undoubtedly the quickest and easiest way to make your rolls and loaves look really special. Creating a beautiful shiny crust, a crunchy topping of seeds and nuts or even adding a brush of your favourite beer can all make a difference to the finished loaf.

When making dough-based recipes adding toppings and glazes is easy – simply brush proved dough with your chosen glaze and bake. Alternatively, for high-sugar glazes apply the glaze once the bread has been removed from the oven. Toppings are best applied after a glaze, as the glaze will help them adhere to the bread.

When using complete breadmaker cycles it's not so obvious when to apply a glaze or topping. The easiest way is to brush the chosen glaze onto the hot loaf after removing it from the bucket at the end of the cycle. The only time I like to lift the lid and add a glaze during the cycle is when using egg-based glazes. Many people have concerns about only eating fully cooked eggs and in this way you can be sure that the glaze will bake along with the bread during the final stage of the cycle.

If your machine's manual gives a breakdown of programme stages you'll be able to see how long your baking cycle is and apply egg and toppings at the appropriate time. If you don't have this information, as a rough guide most machines are baking during the last 45 minutes of the cycle. Take care lifting the lid: the machine is baking – it will be hot and steam is often puffed out. Have everything ready, wear oven gloves and have your glaze at room temperature. To apply, quickly lift the lid, brush on the glaze followed by any topping (if using) and close the lid again.

Like most breadmaker techniques it's all about finding out what works best for you and you'll be able to decide on this using the information in this chapter and the instructions in the handbook accompanying your machine.

glazes

Glazes will add interest to your bread by providing a variety of finishes to the crust. Some glazes will add flavour and some will also vary the texture of the crust. Experiment with some of the ideas on the following pages.

egg wash

For a shiny, golden crust, whisk together 1 egg, 1 tbsp water and a pinch of salt. Brush over proved dough just before baking.

milk

Milk will also give a golden crust if applied before baking. For sweet bread recipes a little sugar can also be added to warm milk and then used as a glaze.

water

For a French-style finish, brush your loaf with warm water at the beginning of the baking cycle. For an intensified effect, you can brush the loaf up to three times during baking, but make sure the crust is dry before brushing on more water otherwise it may go soggy. Also take care when adding water; if it drips onto the hot bucket or the element it will make steam.

salt water

To give a shiny surface and a crisp crust, brush your bread with lightly salted water immediately before the baking cycle.

soya powder and water

Excellent for vegans and a superb egg-free alternative to egg wash. Mix soya powder with water and brush onto proved dough just before the baking cycle.

cornflour and water

For a shiny, chewy crust, use cornflour and water. Simply mix a little cornflour with some water and cook over a low heat until translucent. Cool slightly and apply to bread before baking.

beer

For a rich and shiny crust use your favourite beer, but make sure it's at room temperature.

olive oil

Brushing with olive oil immediately before and again after baking will give a subtle flavour and a rich, shiny crust. I love this on focaccia (see page 80) and traditional flat breads.

butter

Melt a little butter or margarine in the microwave (or over a low heat) and brush over the crust of a cooked loaf (while still hot) to produce a richly flavoured crust with a softer texture.

jam, honey and syrup

Sweet glazes are best applied after baking, directly onto the crust of hot baked bread. Try melted apricot jam flavoured with a sprinkle of cinnamon or runny honey, maple syrup, golden syrup or molasses.

toppings

Toppings will add even more variety to your loaves and are best added immediately after a glaze. Try some of the ideas below.

seeds

There is a wide choice of seeds and seed blends now available at health food stores and supermarkets – use them on both sweet and savoury breads. Whether you choose sunflower, poppy, pumpkin, sesame or caraway, they're best applied after a glaze of egg wash.

grains

Also look in the health food stores at the wide selection of whole and cracked grains that can make a wholesome, rustic topping for savoury breads.

bran

Bran will improve the fibre content of a loaf and also makes a wonderfully textured topping.

oats

Choose from a wide range of different grades and textures, from rolled oats to oatmeal.

flour

For a soft, dusty finish, sift flour over the shaped dough before proving and again before baking.

polenta

Apply a sprinkling of polenta or cornmeal over proved dough brushed with a little water to give a crisp, golden topping.

sugar

For sweet breads, apply an egg glaze (see page 44) and sprinkle lightly with sugar.

salt

Add a continental touch by finishing savoury flat breads with a sprinkling of sea salt.

cheese

Cheese is one of the most popular toppings, but also potentially one of the messiest. I think it's best applied to the finished hot bread and allowed to melt gently. Alternatively, you could add it 5 minutes before the end of the cycle. Parmesan is particularly good applied over a glaze of egg wash or water before baking.

herbs

Don't restrict yourself to dried herbs – use fresh herbs, too. Whether used on flat breads, rolls or loaves, fresh herbs will produce a lovely finish and add both flavour and texture to the finished bread.

bread and butter recipes

- Basic Recipes • French Bread Recipes
  - Blended Flour Recipes
    - A Final Word
    - Flavoured Butters

As there are now so many different breadmakers on the market, it is impossible within the limits of one book to write recipes for the capacity of every machine. All machines have a cycle based on approximately 450 g/16 oz/3 cups of flour and I have used this as a base for all the recipes in this book. Quantities for larger loaves based on 600 g/21 oz/4 cups of flour are also given in the basic recipes and can be found in brackets.

Before starting, see the important note on page 38 regarding the order in which ingredients are added.

basic recipes

classic white bread

With its light, open texture and golden crust, this versatile loaf is perfect for sandwiches and toast.

225 ml/8 fl oz/1 cup (350 ml/12 fl oz/1½ cups) water
2 tbsp (3 tbsp) melted butter, cooled
1½ tbsp (2 tbsp) sugar
1½ tsp (2 tsp) salt
450 g/16 oz/3 cups (600 g/21 oz/4 cups) strong white bread flour
1¼ tsp (2 tsp) instant or fast-acting dried yeast
glaze/topping, to taste (see page 43)

Pour the water into the breadmaker bucket, then add the butter, sugar and salt. Cover with the flour and sprinkle over the yeast. Fit the bucket into the breadmaker and set to the basic white programme for the appropriate size loaf. Once cooked, carefully shake the loaf from the bucket and stand the right way up on a wire cooling rack. Brush with your chosen glaze and add any topping (if using). Leave the bread to cool for at least an hour before cutting and/or removing the paddle if necessary.

soft grain bread

For a versatile white loaf with extra 'bite' provided by the cracked grains added to soft grain flour, follow the recipe for the Classic White Bread (see facing page), replacing the strong white bread flour with soft grain strong white bread flour with kibbled (cracked) grains of rye and wheat.

light wholemeal bread

This is the perfect wholemeal loaf for a breadmaker. It is rich in flavour and lighter in texture than 100 per cent wholemeal bread which I have never found to be acceptable when made in a bread machine.

225 ml/8 fl oz/1 cup (350 ml/12 fl oz/1½ cups) water
3 tbsp (4 tbsp) sunflower oil
2 tbsp (3 tbsp) runny honey
225 g/8 oz/1½ cups (300 g/11 oz/2 cups) strong wholemeal bread flour
1½ tsp (2 tsp) salt
225 g/8 oz/1½ cups (300 g/11 oz/2 cups) very strong white bread flour
1½ tsp (2½ tsp) instant or fast-acting dried yeast
glaze/topping, to taste (see page 43)

Pour the water into the breadmaker bucket and add the oil and honey. Cover the liquid with the wholemeal flour and sprinkle over the salt. Add the white flour and top with the yeast. Fit the bucket into the breadmaker and set to the basic rapid/wholemeal rapid or wholewheat programme for the appropriate size loaf. Once cooked, carefully shake the loaf from the bucket and stand the right way up on a wire cooling rack. Brush with your chosen glaze and add any topping (if using). Leave the bread to cool for at least an hour before cutting and/or removing the paddle if necessary.

light rye bread

With all the flavour of rye, this loaf has a close yet light texture. Try serving it with cold meats and pickles for a taste of the continent. Follow the recipe for Light Wholemeal Bread (see facing page), but replace the wholemeal flour with rye flour.

wholesome white loaf

Wholesome white flour produces a lovely rustic loaf with a golden crust and creamy white, full-flavoured centre. It's the perfect loaf for children who refuse to entertain the idea of brown bread.

> 250 ml/9 fl oz/1⅛ cups (375 ml/13 fl oz/1⅝ cups) water
> 3 tbsp (4 tbsp) sunflower oil
> 2 tbsp (3 tbsp) granulated sugar
> 1½ tsp (2 tsp) salt
> 450 g/16 oz/3 cups (600 g/21 oz/4 cups) wholesome white very strong bread flour
> 1½ tsp (2½ tsp) instant or fast-acting dried yeast
> glaze/topping, to taste (see page 43)

Pour the water into the breadmaker bucket and then add the oil, sugar and salt. Cover with the flour and sprinkle over the yeast. Fit the bucket into the breadmaker and set to the basic white programme for the appropriate size loaf. Once cooked, carefully shake the loaf from the bucket and stand the right way up on a wire cooling rack. Brush with your chosen glaze and add any topping (if using). Leave the bread to cool for at least an hour before cutting and/or removing the paddle if necessary.

country brown bread

A delicious loaf with the distinctive, nutty flavour of brown bread. This bread cuts like a dream and is the perfect accompaniment to both sweet and savoury dishes.

225 ml/8 fl oz/1 cup (350 ml/12 fl oz/1½ cups) water
2 tbsp (3 tbsp) sunflower oil
2 tbsp (3 tbsp) runny honey
1¼ tsp (1½ tsp) salt
450 g/16 oz/3 cups (600 g/21 oz/4 cups) strong brown bread flour
1¼ tsp (2 tsp) instant or fast-acting dried yeast
glaze/topping, to taste (see page 43)

Pour the water into the breadmaker bucket, then add the oil and honey. Cover the liquid with the salt and flour and sprinkle over the yeast. Fit the bucket into the breadmaker and set to the basic white programme for the appropriate size loaf. Once cooked, carefully shake the loaf from the bucket and stand the right way up on a wire cooling rack. Brush with your chosen glaze and add any topping (if using). Leave the bread to cool for at least an hour before cutting and/or removing the paddle if necessary.

malted brown bread

This rustic loaf has all the taste of brown bread with added texture provided by the malted wheat flakes in the flour. It's perfect served sliced or in chunks with everything from soup to cheese.

300 ml/11 fl oz/1⅜ cups (350 ml/12 fl oz/1½ cups) water
2 tbsp (3 tbsp) sunflower oil
½ tbsp (1 tbsp) runny honey
1½ tsp (2 tsp) salt
450 g/16 oz/3 cups (600 g/21 oz/4 cups) country grain strong brown bread flour
1½ tsp (2½ tsp) instant or fast-acting dried yeast
glaze/topping, to taste (see page 43)

Pour the water into the breadmaker bucket, followed by the oil, honey and salt. Cover the wet ingredients with the flour and sprinkle on the yeast. Fit the bucket into the breadmaker and set to the wholewheat/wholemeal programme for the appropriate size loaf. Once cooked, carefully shake the loaf from the bucket and stand the right way up on a wire cooling rack. Brush with your chosen glaze and add any topping (if using). Leave the loaf to cool for at least an hour before cutting and/or removing the paddle if necessary.

lighter malted brown loaf

A lighter, airy loaf but still with enough malted brown flour to give that distinctive flavour and bite. Follow the recipe for Malted Brown Bread (see facing page), but use half country grain strong brown bread flour and half strong white bread flour.

french bread recipes

One of my greatest disappointments when I bought my first bread machine was that the manual only included one standard white French bread recipe. When I saw for myself what this programme could produce, I immediately got to work developing more recipes. We all love buying French bread, whether it's baguettes, sticks or the traditional freeform loaves sold in most supermarkets, and now we can create our own at home. Using a breadmaker means they are shaped like a traditional loaf, but they still have the promise of a crisp crust and that distinctive light and airy centre. However, like all French bread, these loaves are best eaten fresh, on the day they are baked.

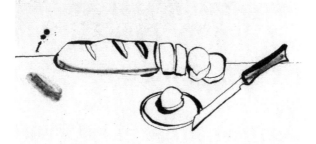

basic french loaf

The classic French-style loaf with a crisp, golden crust and light, airy centre. As this bread contains no fat it stales quickly, so it's best eaten on the day of baking.

> 225 ml/8 fl oz/1 cup water
> 1½ tbsp sugar
> 1½ tsp salt
> 450 g/16 oz/3 cups very strong white bread flour
> 1¼ tsp instant or fast-acting dried yeast
> glaze/topping, to taste (see page 43)

Pour the water into the breadmaker bucket, followed by the sugar and salt. Cover the liquid with the flour and sprinkle over the yeast. Fit the bucket into the breadmaker and set to the French programme. Once cooked, carefully shake the loaf from the bucket and stand the right way up on a wire cooling rack. Brush with your chosen glaze and add any topping (if using). Leave the bread to cool for at least an hour before cutting and/or removing the paddle if necessary.

bread and butter recipes

rustic french bread

The blend of flours gives this bread a wonderfully rustic quality, making it the perfect loaf for al fresco eating.

275 ml/10 fl oz/1¼ cups water
1½ tbsp sugar
1½ tsp salt
70 g/2½ oz/½ cup rye flour
150 g/5¼ oz/1 cup wholesome white very strong bread flour
225 g/8 oz/1½ cups very strong white bread flour
1¼ tsp instant or fast-acting dried yeast
glaze/topping, to taste (see page 43)

Pour the water into the breadmaker bucket, followed by the sugar and salt. Cover the liquid with the flours and sprinkle over the yeast. Fit the bucket into the breadmaker and set to the French programme. Once cooked, carefully shake the loaf from the bucket and stand the right way up on a wire cooling rack. Brush with your chosen glaze and add any topping (if using). Leave the bread to cool for at least an hour before cutting and/or removing the paddle if necessary.

french onion bread

Dried onion flakes give a wonderful flavour to this bread. Add them with the flour and let the machine mash them up while kneading.

250 ml/9 fl oz/1⅛ cups water
2 tsp melted butter, cooled
2 tbsp sugar
2 tsp salt
400 g/14 oz/2¾ cups very strong white bread flour
25 g/1 oz/5 tbsp dried onion flakes
1¼ tsp instant or fast-acting dried yeast
glaze/topping, to taste (see page 43)

Pour the water into the breadmaker bucket and add the butter, sugar and salt. Cover the liquid with the flour. Finally, put the onion flakes on top of the flour at one end of the bucket and the yeast at the other end. Fit the bucket into the breadmaker and set to the French programme. Once cooked, carefully shake the loaf from the bucket and stand the right way up on a wire cooling rack. Brush with your chosen glaze and add any topping (if using). Leave the bread to cool for at least an hour before cutting and/or removing the paddle if necessary.

french garlic and herb bread

This light, airy and aromatic loaf is richly flavoured and has a golden crust and speckled centre. It's perfect served freshly baked and sliced to accompany a hearty winter casserole, or enhance the flavours further by smothering it with home-made garlic and herb butter (see page 71).

225 ml/8 fl oz/1 cup water
2 tbsp olive oil
2 tsp sugar
1 tsp salt
1½ tsp minced dried garlic granules
1½ tsp dried herbes de Provence
450 g/16 oz/3 cups strong white bread flour
1¼ tsp instant or fast-acting dried yeast
glaze/topping, to taste (see page 43)

Pour the water and olive oil into the breadmaker bucket and add the sugar, salt, garlic granules and dried herbs. Cover with the flour and sprinkle on the yeast. Fit the bucket into the breadmaker and set to the French programme. Once cooked, carefully shake the loaf from the bucket and stand the right way up on a wire cooling rack. Brush with your chosen glaze and add any topping (if using). Leave the bread to cool for at least an hour before cutting and/or removing the paddle if necessary.

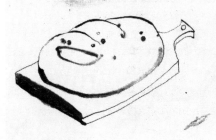

blended flour recipes

Once you have become familiar with baking basic loaves from different bread flours, you can start increasing the variety of breads you make by coming up with your own flour blends. Strong flours can be mixed together to vary both taste and texture and you can have endless fun inventing your own combinations.

For best results, try to stick to a blend comprising at least 50 per cent strong white or wholesome white flour as this will ensure your loaves rise well and retain a light and airy texture. To start you off, here are three of my favourite blended flour recipes.

wholewheat bread with rye

This delicious loaf benefits from the goodness of wholemeal flour and the sweetness provided by a hint of rye. It's great served with cheese.

275 ml/10 fl oz/1¼ cups water
3 tbsp sunflower oil
2 tbsp runny honey
2 tsp salt
150 g/5¼ oz/1 cup wholesome white very strong bread flour
150 g/5¼ oz/1 cup strong wholemeal bread flour
70 g/2½ oz/½ cup rye flour
70 g/2½ oz/½ cup very strong white bread flour
1½ tsp instant or fast-acting dried yeast
glaze/topping, to taste (see page 43)

Pour the water and oil into the breadmaker bucket and add the honey and salt. Cover with the flours and sprinkle on the yeast. Fit the bucket into the breadmaker and set to the basic white programme. Once cooked, carefully shake the loaf from the bucket and stand the right way up on a wire cooling rack. Brush with your chosen glaze and add any topping (if using). Leave the bread to cool for at least an hour before cutting and/or removing the paddle if necessary.

hearty soft grain bread

Soft grain flour gives the texture of rye and wheat grains. When combined with a little rye and wholemeal flours, it makes a versatile loaf.

> 250 ml/9 fl oz/1⅛ cups water
> 2 tbsp sunflower oil
> 2 tbsp runny honey
> 1½ tsp salt
> 70 g/2½ oz/½ cup rye flour
> 70 g/2½ oz/½ cup strong wholemeal bread flour
> 150 g/5¼ oz/1 cup soft grain strong white bread flour
> 150 g/5¼ oz/1 cup strong white bread flour
> 1½ tsp instant or fast-acting dried yeast
> glaze/topping, to taste (see page 43)

Pour the water and oil into the breadmaker bucket and add the honey and salt. Cover with the flours and sprinkle on the yeast. Fit the bucket into the breadmaker and set to the basic white programme. Once cooked, carefully shake the loaf from the bucket and stand the right way up on a wire cooling rack. Brush with your chosen glaze and add any topping (if using). Leave the bread to cool for at least an hour before cutting and/or removing the paddle if necessary.

rustic malt and grain bread

This recipe provides maximum crunch with malted wheat flakes and cracked grains of rye and wheat in a beautifully rich, light brown country loaf.

250 ml/9 fl oz/1⅛ cups water
2 tbsp sunflower oil
1½ tbsp sugar
1½ tsp salt
150 g/5¼ oz/1 cup country grain strong brown bread flour
150 g/5¼ oz/1 cup soft grain strong white bread flour
150 g/5¼ oz/1 cup strong brown bread flour
1½ tsp instant or fast-acting dried yeast
glaze/topping, to taste (see page 43)

Pour the water and oil into the breadmaker bucket and add the sugar and salt. Cover with the flours and sprinkle on the yeast. Fit the bucket into the breadmaker and set to the basic white programme. Once cooked, carefully shake the loaf from the bucket and stand the right way up on a wire cooling rack. Brush with your chosen glaze and add any topping (if using). Leave the bread to cool for at least an hour before cutting and/or removing the paddle if necessary.

a final word

Finally, remember that even though you are using an automatic breadmaker, every loaf will be different. It's part of the charm of home baking. The crust colour and texture will vary, as will its smoothness and shape. If you are having particular problems, refer to the troubleshooting section on page 118. Otherwise, be prepared for variety and enjoy the individual character of your home-made bread.

flavoured butters

What better accompaniment to your bread than a fantastic selection of home-made flavoured butters?

To make flavoured butter, simply cream the soft butter until smooth, beat in the additional ingredients and chill until required. For spreading, allow the butter to come to room temperature before use. For an alternative presentation, form the flavoured butter into a roll and wrap in greaseproof paper. Chill until required and serve in individual slices.

garlic and herb butter

50 g/2 oz butter

1 large clove of garlic, peeled and crushed

2 tsp chopped fresh parsley

1 tbsp lemon juice

salt and freshly ground black pepper

lemon and herb butter

50 g/2 oz butter

grated rind of 1 lemon

2 tsp lemon juice

1 tsp finely chopped fresh parsley

salt and freshly ground black pepper

mustard and mint butter

50 g/2 oz butter

½ tsp Dijon mustard, or to taste

1 tbsp chopped fresh mint

salt and freshly ground black pepper

cinnamon butter

50 g/2 oz butter

1 tbsp icing sugar

1 tbsp ground cinnamon

choc and nut butter

50 g/2 oz butter

1 tsp caster sugar

½ tbsp finely grated chocolate

1 tbsp very finely chopped nuts, e.g. hazelnuts or walnuts

lemon or orange butter

50 g/2 oz butter

1 tbsp icing sugar

grated rind of 1 lemon (or 1 orange)

1 tbsp lemon juice (or orange juice)

making dough

- Making Dough in Your Breadmaker
- Freeform Loaves and Rolls
- Dough Recipes

making dough in your breadmaker

If you've never made dough in your breadmaker, then you're in for a surprise. Forget all that laborious mixing and kneading – the machine will do all this for you and the result is a beautifully smooth, airy dough ready for you to shape, prove and bake in the traditional way.

But why would you want to make dough when the machine makes such fabulous bread, I hear you ask? Well, think of pizzas, beautiful round flat breads brushed with olive oil, croissants and muffins. All of these can be made with ease using the dough cycle plus a little extra time from you to shape the dough and then to finish it off in the conventional way. You'll be amazed at how easy it is to make speciality breads like this – with the hard work done for you, you'll have the time and enthusiasm to experiment with different recipes.

The other great thing I've found about the dough cycle is that if you ever have to amuse children, then fresh bread dough is the answer. It can take no end of bashing, rolling and pulling by a child and still produce something that is edible at the end. And what better way to get children baking than with a popular dish like pizza?

hints for making dough

- In some machines it may be necessary to leave the dough to rise in the bucket even after the programme has finished. Leave it until it has either doubled in size or nearly reached the top of the bucket.
- I always recommend leaving shaped dough to rise slowly at room temperature before baking. As long as it's covered and in a draught-free place it will rise, given time. If, however, time is short you can resort to placing it in the airing cupboard.

Quick Tip

Rising time can be reduced for dough to be baked in the oven only by increasing the amount of yeast: 2½ tsp instant or fast-acting yeast will rise up to 600 g/21 oz/4 cups of flour relatively quickly and without any effect on taste.

- If you want to delay the length of time until your dough is ready to bake, put it in the fridge. Then bring it out and let it finish rising at room temperature before baking.
- For fan ovens, you may need to reduce the baking temperature slightly – usually by about 10–20°C, depending on the recipe.
- For instructions on storing and freezing dough, see page 34.

making dough

freeform loaves and rolls

Basic dough made in the breadmaker can be used as the base for virtually any shape of roll or loaf. Let your imagination run wild and don't forget that toppings and glazes (see page 42) are excellent for adding even more variety.

For freeform loaves and rolls, use any of the basic recipes featured in this book (see pages 52–9) and select the dough cycle. Shape the bread as desired, cover with a clean tea towel and leave to prove until doubled in size (see Quick Tip on page 75). Bake in a conventional oven using the temperatures and timings below for guidance.

dough quantities

As a rough guide, dough made with 450 g/16 oz/3 cups of flour will produce 10–12 bread rolls and dough with 600 g/21 oz/4 cups of flour will make 14–16 rolls (depending on size).

Bread rolls can be baked at 220°C/425°F/gas mark 7 for 10–15 minutes (see note on facing page).

Loaves made from the dough quantities given above will require approximately 25–30 minutes' and 30–35 minutes' baking time respectively in an oven preheated to 220°C/425°F/gas mark 7 and then immediately turned down to 200°C/400°F/gas mark 6 once you put the bread in (see note below). When cooked, loaves and rolls should sound hollow when tapped on the bottom.

note:
When baking in a fan oven, the temperature may need to be reduced by 10–20°C.

roll shapes
The quantities of rolls given below are for dough made with 450 g/ 16 oz/3 cups of flour; for dough made with 600 g/21 oz/4 cups of flour, divide into 14–16 pieces.

In each case, shaped rolls should be placed onto greased baking sheets, covered with a clean tea towel and left to prove until light and puffy. Add any topping or glaze and bake in an oven preheated to 220°C/425°F/gas mark 7 for 10–15 minutes (see note above).

knots
Divide the dough into 12 equally sized pieces and roll each piece into a rope approximately 20 cm/8 in long. Tie the ropes into loose knot shapes.

snails

Divide the dough into 12 equally sized pieces, roll each piece into a 30 cm/12 in rope and form into a coil, tucking the end under.

split tin rolls

Divide the dough into 12 equally sized pieces. Roll each piece into a smooth ball, then shape into an oval. Transfer to greased baking trays and make a lengthwise slit along the top of each roll with a sharp knife, taking care not to cut through to the base.

cloverleaf rolls

Divide the dough into 12 equally sized pieces, then divide each piece into three and shape into a ball. Lightly press the balls together to form a cloverleaf shape.

twists

Divide the dough into 12 equally sized pieces and roll each into a 30 cm/12 in rope. Fold each rope in half and twist. Pinch the ends together to seal.

plaits

Divide the dough into 12 equally sized pieces. Then divide each piece into three and roll into evenly sized ropes. Pinch the ends of the three ropes together and plait the dough, sealing the end and tucking it neatly underneath.

dough recipes

focaccia

Here's my breadmaker adaptation of this traditional Italian hearth bread. Try adding olives, herbs or sundried tomatoes – see the suggested variations on the facing page.

>200 ml/7 fl oz/⅞ cup water
>75 ml/3 fl oz/⅜ cup olive oil
>1½ tsp salt
>1½ tsp sugar
>450 g/16 oz/3 cups very strong white bread flour
>2½ tsp instant or fast-acting dried yeast
>olive oil, to glaze

Pour the water and olive oil into the breadmaker bucket and add the salt and sugar. Cover with the flour and sprinkle over the yeast. Fit the bucket in the breadmaker and set to the dough programme. Once complete, turn the dough onto a floured surface and knead until smooth. Roll out the dough to form a 24 cm/9½ in circle, then place on an oiled baking sheet. Cover with a clean tea towel and leave to prove until double in size. Using your fingertips, dimple the top of the dough to give the distinctive focaccia appearance. Brush with olive oil and bake in an oven preheated to 200°C/400°F/gas mark 6 for 25–30 minutes. Brush again with olive oil while still warm and leave to cool on a wire rack.

variations:
- Brush with olive oil and scatter with sea salt.
- Stud the dough with rosemary or basil leaves before baking.
- Try adding sundried tomatoes or olives to the dough.

making dough

pitta bread

If you've never tried making your own pitta bread I think you'll be surprised just how easy it is, especially as the breadmaker takes all the work out of making the dough.

makes 8

275 ml/10 fl oz/1¼ cups water
½ tsp sugar
1 tsp salt
2 tbsp olive oil
450 g/16 oz/3 cups strong white bread flour
1½ tsp instant or fast-acting dried yeast

Pour the water into the breadmaker bucket, followed by the sugar and salt. Add the olive oil and cover with the flour. Finally sprinkle over the yeast. Fit the bucket into the breadmaker and set to the dough programme. When completed, turn the dough onto a lightly floured surface and knead until smooth. Divide the dough into eight pieces and shape each piece into a ball. Using a rolling pin, roll each ball of dough into a flat oval about 5 mm/¼ in thick. Cover the pittas with a damp tea towel and leave to prove for 15–20 minutes until slightly risen. Meanwhile, preheat the oven to 220°C/425°F/gas mark 7. Dust two baking sheets with flour and place them in the oven to preheat for 5 minutes. Place the pittas on the hot baking sheets and quickly return them to the oven. Cook for 7–10 minutes until puffed up. Once baked, remove from the oven and wrap in a clean tea towel to stop them drying out.

naan bread

You'll be amazed at how quick and easy it is to make your own naan bread. If you want to make the naans ahead of time, simply re-heat them in the oven or for a few seconds in the microwave.

makes 4

250 ml/9 fl oz/1⅛ cups semi-skimmed milk
3 tbsp natural yogurt
1 tsp sugar
1½ tsp salt
2 tbsp melted unsalted butter or ghee
450 g/16 oz/3 cups strong white bread flour
1¼ tsp instant or fast-acting dried yeast

Pour the milk into the breadmaker bucket and add the yogurt, sugar, salt and butter (or ghee). Cover with the flour and sprinkle over the yeast. Fit the bucket into the breadmaker and set to the dough programme. When the cycle is complete, turn the dough onto a lightly floured surface and knead until smooth. Divide the dough into four equally-sized pieces. Roll out each piece of dough into a rectangle about 5 mm/¼ in thick. Preheat the grill to its highest setting and heat a baking sheet under it for a couple of minutes. Cook the naans a couple at a time under the grill for about 2–3 minutes on each side until puffed up and golden. Take care that the dough does not burn. Once cooked, wrap the breads in a clean tea towel to prevent drying out and serve hot.

making dough

french sticks

Crispy on the outside with a moist, chewy centre, these rustic-style French sticks are delicious served at any meal. For an even crisper crust, carefully spray the sticks with water 2–3 times while they are in the oven. A plant mister is an excellent tool for this task.

makes 2–3

300 ml/11 fl oz/1⅜ cups water
1½ tsp salt
1 tsp sugar
450 g/16 oz/3 cups strong white bread flour
1½ tsp instant or fast-acting dried yeast

Pour the water into the breadmaker bucket, followed by the salt and sugar. Cover the liquid with the flour and sprinkle over the yeast. Fit the bucket into the breadmaker and set to the dough programme. Once complete, turn the dough onto a floured board and divide into two or three pieces, depending on the length of sticks your oven will accommodate. Roll each piece of dough into a long thin stick and transfer to lightly greased baking sheets. Cover with a clean tea towel and leave in a warm place to double in size. Brush with water and bake in an oven preheated to 220°C/425°F/gas mark 7 for 15 minutes until crisp and golden.

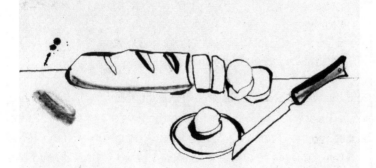

making dough

making pizza

- Making Pizza Dough
- Calzone

making pizza dough

Nothing beats fresh-from-the-oven home-made pizza. And with your breadmaker, delicious home-made pizza is a tasty and convenient option for even the busiest household.

My basic pizza dough recipe can be covered with a variety of assorted toppings to suit all tastes and is sufficient for two 30 cm/ 12 inch pizzas (enough to serve 2–4 people).

If two pizzas are too much for one meal, wrap and freeze the spare one for later – you'll be really glad it's there when you want to put a meal on the table in minutes. If you prefer to keep the dough for another time, wrap it up securely and freeze. When you want to use the dough, ensure that it's defrosted and brought up to room temperature before using it.

basic pizza dough

275 ml/10 fl oz/1¼ cups water
2 tbsp olive oil
2 tsp salt
2 tsp sugar
450 g/16 oz/3 cups strong white bread flour
2½ tsp instant or fast-acting dried yeast

Pour the water into the breadmaker bucket, followed by the olive oil, salt and sugar. Cover with the flour and sprinkle on the yeast. Fit the bucket into the breadmaker and set to the dough programme. Once the cycle is complete, remove the dough from the bucket and quickly knead on a floured surface. Divide the dough in half and roll each piece into a round disc, large enough to cover one (or two) oiled and flour-dusted 30 cm/12 in pizza tins. Cover with sauce and toppings of your choice (see facing page) to within 2.5 cm/1 in of the edge. For a thin crust, refrigerate the prepared pizza for 30 minutes before baking or, for a distinct puffy edge, leave the pizza to rise in the warmth of the kitchen for about 30 minutes. In either case it is important to cover the pizza with a piece of oiled foil to prevent dryness. Preheat the oven to 220°C/450°F/gas mark 7 and bake the pizza for 20–25 minutes.

making pizza

pizza toppings

I think pizza toppings are so personal that it's best to add a sprinkle of this and a handful of that. For this reason I've not given quantities for the topping suggestions below. Once you've made a few pizzas you'll instinctively know the amounts and combinations of ingredients that you like best.

First, spread your pizza with some passata, tomato purée or home-made tomato sauce, then top with any of the following combinations. Finish with extra Mozzarella cheese to taste.

- Chopped fresh oregano, anchovies and Mozzarella
- Sliced fresh tomatoes, freshly crushed garlic, olive oil and oregano
- Sliced fresh tomatoes, fresh basil leaves, Parmesan and Mozzarella
- Pepperoni sausage, sliced peppers and Parmesan
- Sliced mushrooms, fresh oregano, black olives and anchovies
- Sliced fresh chillies, green peppers, red onions and sliced fresh tomatoes
- Crumbled goats' cheese, sun-dried tomatoes and capers
- Thinly sliced potatoes, sliced red onion, Dijon mustard and Emmental
- Pesto, pine nuts and Parmesan

making pizza

- Prawns, feta cheese and black olives
- Sliced mushrooms, green peppers, red onions and sweetcorn
- Roast chicken, sliced mushrooms, yellow peppers and spring onion
- Roast chicken, jalapeños, red onions and a sprinkle of Cajun spice
- Ham slices, sliced pepper and pineapple
- Sautéed leeks, mushrooms, peas and spinach

calzone

Just like pizza, calzone originated as a simple, rustic dish made with whatever ingredients were to hand to make a tasty and practical meal. Literally translated, calzone means 'pocket' or 'trouser sandwich' and is also commonly known as the 'pocket pizza'. Encased in basic pizza dough, calzones are like large golden, puffed turnovers and are shaped rather like Cornish pasties. Made simply by rolling a circle of dough, covering half with the filling, folding over the dough and sealing, calzones quickly made their mark as a tasty, versatile and convenient meal.

Divide one portion of pizza dough (see recipe on page 90) into 4–6 pieces and roll each into a circle about 18 cm/7 in across. Brush the edges with water. Cover half the circle with your filling (see suggestions in the pizza section on pages 91–92, or below), leaving enough uncovered dough at the edge to seal. Fold the dough over the filling to make a semi-circle and press the edges together firmly to seal. Transfer the calzones to greased baking sheets, cover with a clean tea towel and leave to prove for 10 minutes. Brush with olive oil and bake in an oven preheated to 220°C/425°F/gas mark 7 for 10–12 minutes. Then turn the calzones over, brush the other side with oil and bake for a further 10–12 minutes until puffy and golden.

calzone fillings

Just as with pizza any combination of fillings can be used for calzone (see pizza filling suggestions). I prefer to have a little tomato sauce, cubed Mozzarella cheese, spicy sausage, mushrooms and peppers, but you can choose whatever combination appeals to you. For a change, try adding a little ragu sauce (like that used for Bolognaise) instead of tomato sauce. It's best not to make the filling for your calzone too moist otherwise the dough may go soggy.

making pizza

making cakes

- Cake-making in Your Breadmaker
- Cake Recipes

cake-making in your breadmaker

Most breadmakers include a cake cycle and I have found this to be an excellent programme for producing cakes with very little effort. If your machine doesn't have a cake cycle, you may find that your manufacturer's recipe book provides cake recipes that are mixed in the conventional way and then baked in the breadmaker using the 'bake' programme.

As with bread, there are a few handy hints that will help you get the best cakes from your machine. Breadmakers are not suitable for every type of cake, but I have found both moist, light cakes and those laden with fruit and nuts work well.

hints for cake-making

● Generally, cakes are made with a light, batter-like mixture, so you need to scrape down the sides of the bucket with a plastic spatula while the cake is mixing to ensure all ingredients are incorporated.

● It is normal for a cake to only rise a little way up the bucket. Do not try to double-up the quantities given in the recipe otherwise the baking cycle may not be long enough to cook the cake through.

making cakes

- As cakes are high in sugar, I recommend selecting the light crust setting if your machine offers this option on the cake programme.
- Test your cake is cooked before removing it from the machine by carefully inserting a skewer into the centre (taking care not to damage the non-stick surface of the paddle or bucket). If the skewer comes out clean, the cake is cooked. If your cake requires extra cooking refer to the manufacturer's handbook to extend the baking time using the 'bake only' cycle.
- Always leave cakes to cool in the breadmaker bucket for 5–10 minutes before loosening the sides with a plastic spatula and carefully turning out onto a cooling rack.
- Do not use the timer delay setting for making cakes.

cake recipes

banana and cardamom cake

This moist and spicy cake is fragranced with cardamom and enriched with honey and bananas, making it a versatile option for morning coffee, afternoon tea or even a packed lunch.

½ tsp ground cardamom seeds
¼ tsp salt
¾ tsp bicarbonate of soda
1 tsp baking powder
190 g/6½ oz/1¼ cups plain flour
50 ml/2 fl oz/¼ cup water
2 ripe bananas, mashed
2 eggs, beaten
4 tbsp runny honey

Put the cardamom, salt, bicarbonate of soda, baking powder and flour into a bowl and mix together thoroughly. Pour the water into the breadmaker bucket followed by the bananas, eggs and honey. Cover with the flour mixture. Fit the bucket into the breadmaker and set to the cake programme. After 5 minutes lift the lid of the machine and scrape down the sides with a plastic spatula to ensure all the ingredients are incorporated into the mix. Once cooked, leave the cake to stand in the bucket for 5–10 minutes, then carefully shake the cake from the bucket and stand the right way up on a wire cooling rack. Leave to cool for at least an hour before cutting and/or removing the paddle if necessary.

sticky gingerbread

I love gingerbread and, for me, this recipe possesses all the qualities of the best gingerbread. It's moist, sweet, light and sticky and comes with the underlying warmth from the spice – delicious.

125 g/4 oz/½ cup butter
125 g/4 oz/¾ cup soft light brown sugar
50 g/2 oz/⅛ cup golden syrup
75 g/3 oz/³⁄₁₆ cup black treacle
175 g/6 oz/1⅛ cups plain flour
1 tsp ground ginger
1 tsp ground cinnamon
1 tsp bicarbonate of soda
150 ml/5 fl oz/⅝ cup warm semi-skimmed milk
1 medium egg, beaten
1½ tbsp chopped glacé ginger

Put the butter, sugar, syrup and treacle into a saucepan and heat gently (without boiling) until the sugar has dissolved and the butter melted. Pour the treacle mixture into the breadmaker bucket and cover with the flour and spices. Stir the bicarbonate of soda into the warm milk and add this to the mix, together with the beaten egg and ginger. Fit the bucket into the breadmaker and set to the cake programme. After 5 minutes lift the lid of the machine and scrape down the sides with a plastic spatula to ensure all the ingredients are incorporated into the mix. When cooked, remove the bucket from the machine and leave the cake to cool for 5–10 minutes before carefully turning out onto a wire cooling rack.

somerset apple cake

This is a wonderfully moist cake that can also be served as a dessert with thick cream or custard.

450 g/1 lb cooking apples
100 g/3½ oz/⁷⁄₁₆ cup very soft butter
175 g/6 oz/1⅛ cups soft light brown sugar
2 large eggs, beaten
3 tbsp semi-skimmed milk
1 tsp mixed spice
1 tsp ground cinnamon
300 g/11 oz/2 cups self-raising flour
2 tsp baking powder

Peel and core the apples and finely chop the flesh. Put the apple into the breadmaker bucket followed by the other ingredients. Fit the bucket into the breadmaker and set to the cake programme. After 5 minutes lift the lid of the machine and scrape down the sides with a plastic spatula to ensure all the ingredients are incorporated into the mix. When cooked, remove the bucket from the machine and leave the cake to cool for 5–10 minutes before turning out onto a wire rack. Serve cold or warm with thick cream.

date and walnut loaf

This is my easy breadmaker version of this popular classic.

175 ml/6 fl oz/¾ cup boiling water
125 g/4 oz/¾ cup chopped dates
1 tsp bicarbonate of soda
125 g/4 oz/⅝ cup soft margarine
125 g/4 oz/⁹⁄₁₆ cup caster sugar
1 large egg, beaten
250 g/9 oz/1¾ cups plain flour
75 g/3 oz/¾ cup walnut pieces
½ tsp vanilla extract

Pour the boiling water over the dates and bicarbonate of soda and leave them to stand for 10 minutes. Pour the date mixture into the breadmaker bucket and add the remaining ingredients. Fit the bucket into the breadmaker and set to the cake programme. After 5 minutes scrape down the sides of the bucket with a plastic spatula to ensure all the ingredients have been properly incorporated into the mix. When the cycle has finished, remove the bucket from the machine and leave the cake to cool for 5–10 minutes before turning out onto a wire cooling rack.

making cakes

wheat- and gluten-free bread

- Wheat-free Breads
- Gluten-free Diets
- Adapting Recipes for Other Special Diets

Whether through medical necessity or a concern for personal well being, a change in your diet can be hard to manage. And when this change seems to eliminate the base for your toast at breakfast-time, sandwiches at lunchtime, and something to soak up your soup at suppertime, the situation can look bleak.

I've spoken to many people at this point in their lives – people who are desperate for a thread of hope that will reveal how bread, in some form, can still be part of their daily diet. And the truth is it can, albeit made with a different set of ingredients and maybe in a different way. By making bread yourself, you have complete control over the ingredients and you can produce many breads that will allow both toast and sandwiches to remain part of daily life.

wheat-free breads

For many people, a wheat-free diet initially seems to eliminate completely the chance of ever eating bread again. However, with the wide choice of alternative flours available at supermarkets, health food stores and via the internet, there's a lot of scope for tasty alternatives. The main consideration here is that without the strong gluten structure provided by wheat, making loaves on a complete breadmaker cycle with some flours is not possible. However, there is nothing to stop you using the dough cycle to mix and knead, then removing the dough and finishing the loaf in the conventional way.

The one exception is spelt. Spelt is a grain that is closely related to wheat. However, it's been found that many individuals who cannot tolerate wheat can eat spelt. If in any doubt, check with your GP or dietician that spelt is suitable for your needs. If it is, then wheat-free breads on complete breadmaker cycles are a viable alternative.

In addition, as the gluten-free recipes have to preclude wheat, these would also be relevant for a wheat-free diet (see page 106).

spelt bread

Spelt is a grain that, while closely related to wheat, can be tolerated by some people following a wheat-free diet. It makes a beautiful light brown loaf perfect for all occasions.

> 225 ml/8 fl oz/1 cup water
> 1 tbsp sugar
> 1½ tbsp sunflower oil
> ¾ tsp salt
> 450 g/16 oz/3 cups spelt flour
> 2¼ tsp instant or fast-acting dried yeast
> glaze/topping, to taste (see page 43)

Put the water, sugar, oil and salt into the breadmaker bucket. Cover with the flour and sprinkle over the yeast. Fit the bucket into the breadmaker and set to the basic white programme. Once cooked, carefully shake the loaf from the bucket and stand the right way up on a wire cooling rack. Brush with your chosen glaze and add any topping (if using). Leave the bread to cool for at least one hour before cutting and/or removing the paddle if necessary.

wheat- and gluten-free bread

gluten-free diets

Gluten intolerance or coeliac disease has been diagnosed in about 50,000 people in the UK, although it's estimated that a further 500,000 could have the condition without being aware of it. A gluten-free diet means that grains such as wheat, barley, spelt, kumat, rye, and oats, and their products bran, wheatgerm, semolina, durum, bulghar and couscous, must all be strictly avoided.

Despite the elimination of many grains, people on a coeliac diet can usually eat the following flours which don't contain gluten: potato, rice, corn, buckwheat, tapioca, chickpea (channa), gram, millet, quinoa, soya and arrowroot, together with their products such as cornmeal and polenta.

gluten-free bread

Gluten-free bread flour is now widely available in most supermarkets and health food shops. Some brands already contain a substance called xanthum gum (although you can buy this separately and add it to your own flour combinations if you wish). Like live yoghurt and the friendly bacteria drinks now on the market, xanthum gum is made from a bacterium and works wonderfully to give improved rise, texture and mouth-feel to gluten-free bread and cakes. Xanthum gum is an excellent ingredient for gluten-free baking and is available from larger supermarkets and health food stores.

Quick Tip

Xanthum gum does not mix well with water, so always mix it thoroughly with the flour or dry ingredients before adding to the breadmaker bucket.

Unlike wheat bread, gluten-free breads are made from a mix that resembles a very thick batter rather than a traditional dough. Because of the lack of elasticity in the mix, it's necessary to scrape down the edges of the bucket with a plastic spatula during the mixing cycle to ensure all the ingredients are fully incorporated into the batter mix prior to baking.

A lot of the latest breadmakers now have specific cycles for gluten-free loaves and I have found these to be very good. If you are following a gluten-free diet, a machine with this particular option would be the best choice for you.

Expect your gluten-free loaves to have a different texture to traditional wheat breads. They will not rise as high and will have a moist, firm, cake-like texture.

wheat- and gluten-free bread

gluten-free white bread

A basic recipe to which you can add fruits, seeds and nuts according to your taste and dietary requirements.

300 g/11 oz/2 cups rice flour
150 g/5¼ oz/1 cup potato starch (farina)
150 g/5¼ oz/1 cup tapioca flour
1 tbsp xanthum gum
1½ tsp salt
225 ml/8 fl oz/1 cup water
1 tsp cider vinegar
3 tbsp runny honey
2 large eggs, beaten (approx. 125 ml/4 fl oz/½ cup in volume)
50 ml/2 fl oz/¼ cup sunflower oil
125 ml/4 fl oz/½ cup rice milk
3 tsp instant or fast-acting dried yeast

Carefully measure the three flours into a bowl and add the xanthum gum and salt. Stir to blend all the ingredients together. Pour the water into the breadmaker bucket and add the vinegar, honey, eggs, oil and milk. Cover the liquid with the flour mixture and sprinkle over the yeast. Fit the bucket into the breadmaker and set to the gluten-free/quick bread or cake programme. Lift the lid as the dough is mixing and scrape down the sides of the bucket with a plastic spatula to ensure all the ingredients are incorporated. Once cooked, carefully shake the loaf from the bucket and stand the right way up on a wire cooling rack. Leave the loaf to cool for at least one hour before cutting and/or removing the paddle if necessary.

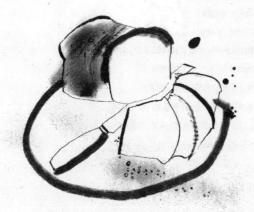

parmesan bread with olives and pumpkin seeds

This loaf is cleverly flavoured to make the perfect gluten- and wheat-free accompaniment to Italian food and salads. Or try using it for your favourite sandwich.

375 g/13 oz/2½ cups gluten-free white bread flour
70 g/2½ oz/½ cup gram flour
1 tsp xanthum gum
225 ml/8 fl oz/1 cup water
1 tsp cider vinegar
1 large egg, beaten
50 ml/2 fl oz/¼ cup olive oil
1½ tbsp runny honey
1½ tsp salt
25 g/1 oz/⅛ cup pumpkin seeds
50 g/2 oz/⅜ cup pitted green olives, sliced
50 g/2 oz/⅝ cup finely grated Parmesan cheese
3 tsp instant or fast-acting dried yeast
glaze/topping, to taste (see page 43)

In a bowl mix together the two flours and the xanthum gum. Pour the water into the breadmaker bucket, followed by the vinegar, egg and oil. Add the honey, salt, seeds, olives and cheese. Cover with the flour mixture and sprinkle over the yeast. Fit the bucket into the breadmaker and set to the gluten-free or quick bread programme. When cooked, carefully shake the loaf from the bucket and cool on a wire rack the right way up. Brush with your chosen glaze and add any topping (if using). Leave to cool for at least one hour before slicing and/or removing the paddle.

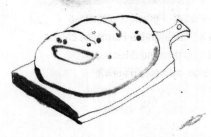

mascarpone, orange and raisin tea bread

Rich and fruity and perfect for afternoon tea, this wonderful gluten-free loaf will be loved by everyone.

190 g/6½ oz/1¼ cups rice flour
100 g/3½ oz/¾ cup tapioca flour
100 g/3½ oz/¾ cup potato starch
1 tbsp xanthum gum
1½ tsp salt
4 tbsp demerara sugar
100 g/3½ oz/¾ cup raisins
50 ml/2 fl oz/¼ cup water
1 tsp cider vinegar
2 large eggs, beaten
50 ml/2 fl oz/¼ cup melted butter
125 ml/4 fl oz/½ cup semi-skimmed milk
100 g/3½ oz/⅜ cup mascarpone cheese
grated zest of 1 orange
juice of 1 orange (approx. 75 ml/3 fl oz/⅜ cup)
3 tsp instant or fast-acting dried yeast
glaze/topping, to taste (see page 43)

In a bowl mix together the two flours, potato starch, xanthum gum, salt, sugar and raisins. Pour the water into the breadmaker bucket and add the vinegar, eggs, butter, milk, cheese, orange zest and juice. Cover with the flour mixture and sprinkle over the yeast. Fit the bucket into the breadmaker and set to the gluten-free/quick bread programme. Lift the lid of the machine as the dough is mixing and scrape down the sides of the bucket with a plastic spatula to ensure all the ingredients are incorporated into the dough. When cooked, carefully shake the loaf from the bucket and cool on a wire rack the right way up. Brush with your chosen glaze and add any topping (if using). Leave to cool for at least one hour before slicing and/or removing the paddle if necessary.

adapting recipes for other special diets

How to cut down or cut out different ingredients from your diet.

dairy

Simply replace any milk used in bread recipes with water or a non-dairy milk alternative, e.g. soya or rice milk. Similarly, butter can be replaced with oil or a non-dairy fat designed for baking.

eggs

Either choose a bread recipe without egg or use a cholesterol-free egg substitute (available from health food shops) in the recipes, following the manufacturer's instructions given on the pack.

sugar

Keep this one in perspective. Remember that bread itself is a relatively low-sugar food, so the first point to make is that you are probably better off cutting down on the sugar contained in what you eat on it or with it, e.g. jam and marmalade.

I use the minimum amount of sugar in recipes wherever possible within the limits of breadmaker cycles, and in some cases honey is used as a more natural alternative. Technically, bread will rise without sugar as the yeast will eventually feed on the starch in the flour, breaking it down to glucose, but this does not happen quickly so you cannot omit sugar from breads made in a breadmaker. If you are adamant about omitting sugar altogether, use the dough cycle and leave the dough to rise very slowly, then bake in the traditional way.

salt

In general, cutting down on salt added to food is relatively simple to do. In bread, however, it can be tricky as salt regulates the action of yeast. Ideally, it's best simply to cut salt to the minimum in bread rather than cutting it out completely. Remember, while a couple of teaspoons of salt may go into a loaf, a slice of bread will contain only a fraction of this. Using some salt is especially important when baking in a breadmaker, where the machine strictly regulates rising and proving times. Omitting salt may lead to breads either rising out of control or falling in on themselves. For best results, try turning your attention to cutting out the salt in what you put on the bread rather than in it.

fat

Remember that bread is not a high fat food; it's usually what you put on it that makes the difference. However, for the benefit of those who want no added fat or oil in their loaves, I recommend trying French bread recipes (see pages 60–5) as these generally contain no fat or oil; the downside is that without fat the bread does not keep well, so this bread will need to be eaten on the day it is baked.

step-by-step troubleshooting

- The Ten Most Frequently Asked Questions
- Troubleshooting Guide

Q: My breadmaker's instruction book says I should use dried yeast in my breadmaker, but there are many different ones on the market – which yeast should I use?

A: Always use instant, fast-acting or easy-bake yeast in your breadmaker. This yeast does not require any reconstituting before adding to the mix. Therefore, it activates quickly once the dough starts mixing, ensuring that you'll get the best possible rise within the limits of the breadmaker cycles.

Instant, fast-acting or easy-bake yeast is available in sachets and larger vacuum packs from all good supermarkets.

Never use fresh yeast or traditional dried active yeast (usually sold in tins) in your breadmaker. For more information see page 29.

Q: My manufacturer's recipe book only gives ingredients in cups and I find it difficult to measure all my ingredients in this way, especially things like butter and cheese. Can you help?

A: Measuring your ingredients carefully and accurately is one of the golden rules of baking with a breadmaker and many people find it difficult to adopt the cup measure. When using a cup, simply level all dry ingredients off with the back of a knife – there's no need to press them down into the cup. The only things that need to be compressed into the cup are ingredients with a paste-like consistency, such as butter or cream cheese, to ensure that there are no air pockets. For best results when measuring liquids, let the cup settle on a flat, level surface, then crouch down to read the level horizontally.

If you are really finding cups difficult, use recipes which give the standard gram and ounce measures. For more information see page 136.

Q: I love wholemeal bread and have tried to make this in my breadmaker but it comes out too dense and heavy to eat. What am I doing wrong?

A: Quite simply, in my opinion, dough made with all strong wholemeal flour will not produce acceptable results if made on a complete breadmaker cycle. While many manufacturers' handbooks give recipes for 100 per cent wholemeal loaves, I've never been satisfied with the quality of the results. I recommend using a blend of 50 per cent strong wholemeal flour and 50 per cent strong white or very strong white bread flour to give your loaf a better rise and lighter texture. If you are insistent on using 100 per cent wholemeal flour only, choose the dough programme, then rise and bake the bread in the traditional way. For more information see page 74.

Q: **I have been using the overnight timer on my breadmaker but keep waking up in the morning to a loaf that has hardly risen. I've checked that I'm using the right yeast and that it's within its use-by date and I understand that the water must not be added too hot – what else could I be doing wrong?**

A: It seems likely that the yeast is coming into contact with the liquid during the night before the machine is programmed to start mixing the dough. Consequently, there's no power left in the yeast to rise the bread.

Ingredients must always be added in the order specified by your particular machine's manufacturer, as this will naturally keep the yeast well away from any moisture. Always make sure that the flour acts as a buffer, keeping the yeast and liquid completely separate otherwise the yeast will be activated too early and will be inactive by the time the delayed cycle begins. For more information see page 38.

Q: I follow a healthy lifestyle and like to keep my salt and sugar intake to a minimum. Can I leave the salt and sugar out of my breadmaker recipes?

A: The quick answer here is no! In breadmaker recipes, in particular, salt is essential to control the action of the yeast and, in turn, stops the bread rising out of control. Similarly, a little sugar is needed to kick-start the yeast into action and to ensure an adequate rise within the timed limits of breadmaker cycles.

Consider this: most standard loaves only contain a couple of teaspoons of salt and only a little more sugar. Once the loaf is sliced, the actual amount of salt and sugar per serving will only be a fraction of this amount. My advice is always to concentrate on reducing the salt and sugar in what you put on your bread or serve with it. For more information see pages 31 and 32.

Q: I've tried several recipes in my manufacturer's handbook without success; my loaves are either poorly risen and dense or sunken and soggy in the middle. Having looked at the fault-finding section in my handbook, it seems my dough is either too dry or too wet – how do I overcome this?

A: While breadmakers are fully automatic, they can only work with the combination of ingredients that we give them. Careful measuring is the key (see page 37). Consider, also, that seasonal changes in humidity, or indeed whether or not you have your central heating turned on, can also affect the absorbency of the flour you use. Obviously in dry weather, your flour will be drier and will need more water to make a pliable dough, and vice versa in more humid weather conditions.

The only way to be certain that your dough is the right consistency to make a well-risen loaf is to check it during the cycle. Do not be afraid to lift the lid of the machine while the dough is mixing or kneading. Look at the dough, feel it and listen to the sound of the machine as it is working. It may be that you need to add a little more liquid or flour during the kneading cycle to make an elastic and pliable consistency. If you do this, any fluctuations in the consistency can be rectified before the rising cycles, ensuring good results every time. For more information see page 39.

Also, follow only one basic recipe until consistently good results have been achieved. If you look at your dough as advised you'll quickly learn what the right consistency should be for a well risen loaf that suits your own personal taste.

Q: **I bought a breadmaker because I wanted to control the ingredients that went into my bread. My local mill produces a range of organic bread flours and I've tried these several times on my basic and wholewheat cycles, but I find the loaves are dense and heavy. Can you help?**

A: Unfortunately, in my experience, organic bread flours do not tend to produce a strong enough gluten structure for dough to rise effectively within the strict time limits of breadmaker cycles. So the best advice is to either use regular (non-organic) bread flour if making dough on complete cycles or to use the dough cycle only when baking with organic flours and then to rise and bake the bread in the traditional way.

Q: I have made successful loaves in my breadmaker for many months but since returning from holiday cannot seem to get my bread to rise at all. What could be going wrong?

A: As you have had consistent success in the past and presumably have not changed any ingredients at all, I would suggest checking the use-by date on your flour and yeast? Were you using up the remains of an opened yeast sachet? It may be that your yeast has become inactive in which case a new pack may simply be the answer (see page 30).

Q: My breadmaker has so many programmes that I'm confused as to which one to use for my wholemeal bread which I make with a 50:50 blend of strong wholemeal and strong white flour. Should I use the wholewheat programme rather than the basic white cycle?

A: Don't worry too much about which programme should be used. Simply choose the programme recommended in your recipe. Generally most lighter wholemeal loaves made with at least 50 per cent strong white flour in the mix will rise and bake happily on the basic, white cycle. If you'd like a loaf that rises slightly more, you can try the wholewheat cycle as generally these cycles have a longer rising time more suited to denser, heavier doughs. For more information on the differences between breadmaker programmes see page 18.

Q: I would like to adapt some of my mother's bread recipes so that I can make them in my breadmaker. I've read in my handbook that I should not exceed the total amount of flour to ensure loaves don't overload my machine, but how do I convert the quantities of fresh yeast to easy-bake yeast?

A: As a rule of thumb:

For converting from fresh yeast:

25 g (1 oz) of fresh yeast is equivalent to 7 g (¼ oz) or 2½ tsp (1 sachet) of instant/fast-acting/easy-bake yeast.

For converting from traditional dried active yeast:

15 g (½ oz) traditional dried active yeast is equivalent to 7 g (¼ oz) or 2½ tsp (1 sachet) of instant/fast-acting/easy-bake yeast.

troubleshooting guide

If you're not entirely satisfied with your loaf, use the following troubleshooting guide to help you. See also the important recipe notes on page 139.

dough/mixing

The dough is crumbly and does not form a soft ball
There is insufficient liquid in the dough. Add more liquid 1 tbsp at a time during the kneading cycle until a soft dough is formed.

The dough is very sticky and does not form a ball
The dough is too wet. Add a little flour 1 tbsp at a time, waiting for the flour to be fully absorbed before adding more.

The dough has not mixed or only partially mixed
Either you forgot to fit the paddle into the bucket or the paddle was not fixed properly into the shaft. Alternatively, the bucket was not correctly fitted into the machine.

rising

My bread rises too much

This could be due to the following reasons:

- There is too much yeast in the recipe – try reducing the yeast by ¼ tsp next time.
- There is too much sugar or sweet ingredients in the recipe.
- You may have forgotten to add salt to the dough.
- The recipe used may contain too much dough volume for the capacity of your machine. Check the recipe quantities match the amount of flour recommended for a loaf in your manufacturer's handbook.

The bread does not rise enough

Again, there are a number of problems that can cause this situation:

- There is not enough yeast in the dough.
- The yeast may be inactive or out of date.
- Was the yeast killed off because the liquid was too hot when you added it to the bucket?
- The yeast and salt came into contact with each other prior to the dough mixing.

- If you chose a rapid cycle, the bread may not have had sufficient time to rise.
- No sugar or sweet ingredients were added. Yeast needs some sugar to feed it; however, too much will retard the yeast.
- There was too much salt in the recipe. You may have used a tbsp measure rather than a tsp, or added the salt twice.
- Did you use strong bread flour in the recipe?
- Remember bread made with heavier flours like wholemeal and rye will not rise as high as their white equivalents and, unless they are mixed with strong white flour, will not produce satisfactory loaves in a breadmaker.
- If the dough was too dry it would also not rise properly. Dough needs to be soft and pliable for a good rise.

The bread did not rise at all

No yeast was added. Or the yeast added was either inactive, killed off by other ingredients being too hot, or was past its use-by date.

baking

The bread has mixed but not baked

The dough cycle was selected. Either remove the dough from the bucket and bake in the oven, or bake it in the machine if you have a bake-only cycle.

There is a burning smell and smoke is coming from the machine

Ingredients or dough have been spilt on the heating element. Wipe the machine out with a damp cloth once it is cold.

finished loaf

The loaf has collapsed

The bread has collapsed after rising or during baking. There are a number of factors that can produce this result:

- The dough was too wet. Either reduce the liquid by 1–2 tbsp next time or add a little more flour.
- There was too much yeast in the mixture. Reduce the amount of yeast slightly next time.

- Not enough salt was added to control the action of the yeast.
- High humidity or warm weather can cause the dough to collapse for no apparent reason.
- The dough may have contained a high proportion of cheese or too much fresh onion or garlic.

My bread is not baked in the centre or on top

There can be several reasons for this:
- The dough was too wet because too much liquid was added. Add less liquid next time and check the dough when mixing, making any necessary adjustments during the kneading cycle.
- The quantities for the recipe were too much for your machine and it could not bake the loaf effectively.
- The dough was too rich. It may have contained too much fat, sugar or eggs.

The bread has a holey texture

- Either the dough was too wet or the salt was omitted from the dough.
- Warm weather or high humidity can also cause the dough to rise too quickly.

The crust of my loaf is too chewy and tough

Slightly increase the fat content of the loaf by adding a little more butter, oil or milk.

The crust is shrivelled

If the crust is shrivelled or wrinkled, moisture has condensed on the top of the cooked loaf. Remove the bread from the machine as soon as the cycle has finished.

The loaf has a burnt crust

There could be too much sugar in the dough. Use less sugar or try the 'light' crust setting next time. The sweet bread setting will also be better for producing a lighter crust.

The loaf is very pale

Choose from the following solutions:

- Add milk, either dried or fresh, to the dough as this encourages browning.
- Select the dark crust option if your machine has one.
- Increase the sugar content slightly.
- Experiment with different glazes (see page 44).

The bread has a crumbly, coarse texture

Either the bread rose too much or the dough was too dry. Either reduce the amount of yeast slightly next time or add more liquid to make a more pliable dough.

Not evenly mixed (flour and added ingredient deposits)

- Added ingredients were chopped up instead of remaining whole.
- The ingredients were added at the beginning of the cycle. Add ingredients like fruit and nuts when the machine bleeps or towards the end of the second kneading cycle (see instructions in your manufacturer's handbook). Also try leaving fruit and nuts in larger pieces when they are added.
- Added ingredients were added too late in the kneading cycle. Add them a little earlier next time.

There are deposits of flour on the sides of the loaf

Sometimes dry ingredients like flour can stick to the sides of the bucket during kneading and then stick unmixed to the risen dough. Check the dough during the mixing cycle and carefully scrape down the sides of the bucket with a plastic spatula to ensure all the flour is fully incorporated.

The bread is dry

● The bread was left uncovered to cool for too long and has dried out, or the bread has been stored in the fridge.

● Breads low in fat or made on the French bread cycle dry out very quickly and are best eaten on the day they are baked.

The bread is difficult to cut and squashes easily when sliced, and the slices are doughy and tacky

Either the bread was cut straight away after being baked or was not allowed sufficient time to cool before slicing.

conversion charts

- *Measurement Conversions*
- *Important Notes*

measurement conversions

The conversions provided here are for flour only and are based on the 225 ml/8 fl oz plastic cup measure supplied with most bread machines. These conversions will NOT be applicable to other dry ingredients as 1 cup of flour will weigh a different amount to 1 cup of walnuts or 1 cup of grated cheese. Therefore, the chart below should ONLY be used for flour. (Liquid conversions are given on page 138.)

flour conversions only

25 g	1 oz	
50 g	2 oz	
70 g	2½ oz	½ cup
75 g	3 oz	⅝ cup
100 g	3½ oz	
125 g	4 oz	⅞ cup
150 g	5¼ oz	1 cup
175 g	6 oz	
190 g	6½ oz	1¼ cups
200 g	7 oz	
225 g	8 oz	1½ cups

250 g	9 oz	1¾ cups
275 g	10 oz	
300 g	11 oz	2 cups
350 g	12 oz	
375 g	13 oz	2½ cups
400 g	14 oz	2¾ cups
425 g	15 oz	
450 g	16 oz/1 lb	3 cups
475 g	17 oz	
500 g	17½ oz	3½ cups
525 g	18½ oz	
550 g	19½ oz	
575 g	20 oz	3⅞ cups
600 g	21 oz	4 cups

conversion charts

liquid conversions only

25 ml	1 fl oz	⅛ cup
50 ml	2 fl oz	¼ cup
75 ml	3 fl oz	⅜ cup
125 ml	4 fl oz	½ cup
150 ml	5 fl oz	⅝ cup
175 ml	6 fl oz	¾ cup
200 ml	7 fl oz	⅞ cup
225 ml	8 fl oz	1 cup
250 ml	9 fl oz	1⅛ cups
275 ml	10 fl oz	1¼ cups
300 ml	11 fl oz	1⅜ cups
350 ml	12 fl oz	1½ cups
375 ml	13 fl oz	1⅝ cups
400 ml	14 fl oz	1¾ cups
425 ml	15 fl oz	1⅞ cups
450 ml	16 fl oz	2 cups

conversion charts

important notes

- Measure your ingredients carefully. Take time to allow liquid to settle in the measure and read from the side on a level surface. For flour, level the surface but do not squash the flour into the cup.

- Always use the plastic spoon measure supplied with your bread machine for all tsp and tbsp measuring. NEVER use household cutlery as these vary greatly in capacity and can lead to inaccurate measuring of ingredients and poor results.

- If you prefer to use grams and ounces, invest in a set of digital scales to measure ingredients for your bread-making. Most of these scales will measure both wet and dry ingredients.

- Use one set of measures only; never mix metric, imperial or cups in the same recipe.

- Always check that the total amount of flour in a recipe is the same as the total amount recommended in your manufacturer's handbook. If your machine makes different sizes of loaf, check which setting is applicable for the chosen recipe.

conversion charts

further reading

Also by Karen Saunders and published by Ebury Press:

The Breadmaker Bible
Traditional Breads for your Breadmaker

index

index